Espen Markussen

Wrap It Up

100S OF FAST, FUN, AND FESTIVE GIFT WRAPPING IDEAS

St. Martin's Griffin New York

WRAP IT UP. Copyright ©
2008 by Cappelen Damm AS.
Translation copyright © 2009
by St. Martin's Press. All rights
reserved. Printed in China. For
information, address St. Martin's
Press, 175 Fifth Avenue, New
York, N.Y. 10010.

www.stmartins.com

Library of Congress Cataloging-
in-Publication Data Available
Upon Request

ISBN 978-0-312-57482-6

First published in Norway by
Cappelen Damm

First U.S. Edition: October 2009

10 9 8 7 6 5 4 3 2 1

Contents

Foreword

Gift wrapping is a tradition all over the world, but with our busy lives today, fewer and fewer of us take the time to add that little extra flourish to the gifts we wrap for friends and family. With this book, I hope to inspire you with many great ideas for transforming even the simplest gift into something special and unique that says you care about and appreciate the recipient.

When looking for inspiration, start in your own home. What kinds of materials do you already have on hand? Traditional wrapping paper and bows are just a beginning. Consider unusual paper like maps, art posters, cellophane, and newspaper. Or why not glue die-cut scrapbooking motifs to the paper or make a collage from various photographs? Instead of bows, you can use wire, leather straps, belts, dog collars, or scarves. Collect papers, remnants from rolls of tape, ribbons, boxes, and gift bags. Everything can be decorated—and anything can be used as a decoration. My goal is to make wrapping gifts almost as much fun as opening them.

Let your imagination run wild and give your gift wrap a personal, heartwarming touch.

Acknowledgements
I want to thank my friends, who have always been inspiring and honest—especially Fredrik, Hilde, and Anki, whom I can always trust and who are never more than a phone call away. And thank you to Synne, my "old" teacher, who taught me that anyone can be exactly what they want to be, and that you are never too old to play. .

Espen Markussen (b. 1978) is a designer from Nøtterøy in Vest-fold, Norway. He is the head of his own design firm: E-Design. He has also been part-owner of an art and hobby supply store for many years. Espen studied graphic design and marketing and he enjoys working creatively with his hands.

True love

Supplies: Wrapping papers – Ribbons – Small D-rings – Strings of beads – Paper or silk flowers – Loose pearls – Thin wire –Gift tags –Tape – Scissors – Glue gun & glue

Simple is often best—even when you're wrapping bridal gifts. I wrapped the lavender package in hand-printed paper and bound it with two velvet-ribbon "belts" fastened with simple silver D-rings. To make a belt, cut the ribbon longer than needed and glue one end around one D-ring. Wrap the ribbon around the package, slip another D-ring over the free end of the ribbon, and then cinch that end through both D-rings. Sophisticated.

Mix plain paper in any color you like with a fancier set of ribbons. I added several narrow velvet ribbons and some strands of beads in harmonizing hues to two of these pale golden-color packages. I

wrapped ribbon around one box in both directions and added some paper roses. Beautiful, isn't it?

The butterfly trimming is simply a classic bow tied with two pairs of loops. I first glued the ribbon to the package, ending with the loose ends on the top, and then tied the bow. To make the butterfly body, I strung some loose pearls on a longish piece of wire, which I wrapped around the bow and twisted closed. Then for the antennae, I separated the wire ends, added a pearl to each, and shaped each in a spiral. A string of pearls lightly glued to the wrapped ribbon adds an extra flourish. You could try this in other colors—whatever suits the recipient.

Tip

Light-colored paper goes well
with any kind of ribbon.

Go nuts

Supplies: Gift boxes with dish-like lids – Pistachio nuts –
Raffia – Ribbons – Cords – Scissors – Gift tags –
Glue gun & glue

Aren't these presents dreamy? I bought the boxes especially for
this purpose. Each has an indentation in the middle of the lid that
helps to keep small objects in place when you glue them. I decided
to leave the boxes unpainted and let the pistachio nuts take center
stage. Glue the nuts close together in the middle of the lid, and tie
raffia and a complementary ribbon or cord around the box. I think
the pale green color I used here is a treat for the eye. .

Tip : Instead of nuts, use beads,
flowers, or whatever sparks
your imagination.

For Mother
From Espen

For Mother

For Bennett
From Katherine

Tip Stores that sell wallpaper usually give away the
old sample books when the season is over!

Ahh, fragrance!

Supplies: Wallpapers – Dried fruit, flowers, or similar natural materials – Jute cord –
Gift tags – Scissors – Glue gun & glue

These gifts are wrapped in some old wallpaper I had lying around. Wallpaper makes fantastic wrapping paper, and it comes in every color and texture imaginable; I think stone and bark effects are great for this gift wrap. The dried flowers and fruits—which I prepared myself—add a lovely fragrance. Once you've glued the wallpaper in place, wrap the package with jute cord or a similar rustic binding, and then simply tuck the dried elements in between the cords. Intriguing natural materials give true character to these packages. You may like to experiment with pinecones, leaves, or other things you find outdoors. .

Great gift boxes
for summer parties

Supplies: Chipwood boxes with lids – Acrylic paint & paintbrush – Ribbons –
Paper or fabric butterflies – Felt flower cutouts – Scissors – Glue gun & glue

Colorful painted boxes with lift-off lids are an ingenious wrapping for a gift that has lots of small pieces.
Even better, the recipient can use the boxes later for other things. If you use a set of graduated boxes,
paint each a different color; then fill, stack, and bind them with complementary ribbons tied in a big, floppy
bow with streamers. I chose three of my favorite colors for this set of boxes; I'm sure you have favorites
too. For summer, I like to glue faux butterflies and fun felt flower cutouts to the ribbons.

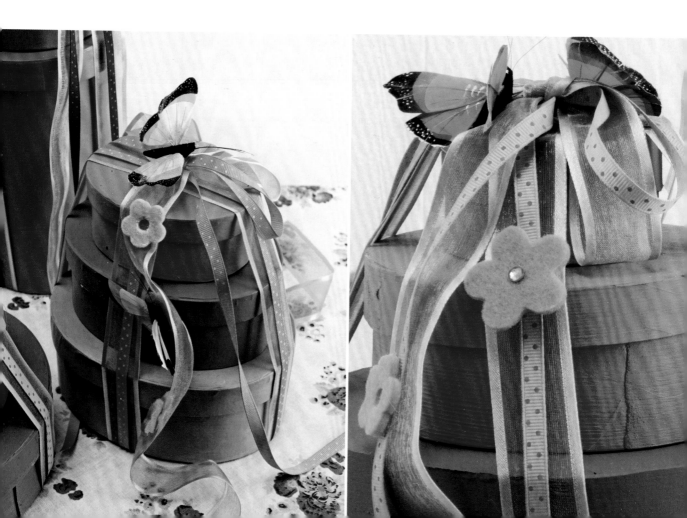

Best wishes

Supplies: Wrapping paper – Ribbon – Cord – Small heart cutouts – Scissors – Tape – Glue gun & glue

Here is a gift wrap everyone will think is elegant and unique! Done in silvery hues like this, it's the perfect presentation for a wedding gift of silverware, with a few pieces tied on top to hint at more inside. I made a coordinating gift tag from solid-colored paper. To finish the package, I glued small silver heart cutouts to the cord and ribbon..

Be Happy!

Field of flowers

Supplies: Wrapping paper – Corrugated paper – Fleece cord – Gift tags – Scissors –
Tape – Glue gun & glue

If you use the right paper, a beautiful present can be as simple as one, two, three: Wrap with paper, add a strip of corrugated paper, and tie with a fleece cord. That's it. Of course, a gift tag finishes it off..

Green is the color of hope

Supplies: Wrapping paper – Thin ribbon – Felt flower cutouts –
Pearls – Gift tags – Scissors – Tape – Glue gun & glue

For a pretty yet tailored effect, wrap your package and then add neatly folded bands of the same paper to it. You can pleat one piece of paper to create the bands, or make each individually and overlap them when you place them. Here I've tied a very thin ribbon .over each band and then glued a felt flower cutout topped with a small pearl to each bow. You'll see other ways to use this idea on pages 21 and 22..

To Britt
From Amy

Tip

Instead of using readymade paper flowers, you can use a die-cutting machine to make other shapes.

Pink, red, black & white!

Supplies: Patterned & plain wrapping papers – Angel-hair tissue paper – Wide mesh ribbon – Corrugated paper – Thin ribbons – Cords – Small paper flowers – Large felt flower – Small glass beads – Small flower jewels – Rubber stamps & ink pads – Scissors – Tape – Glue gun & glue

For these packages I mixed plain, patterned, and textured elements to create some excitement. You could make the wide bands from mesh ribbon, fancy tissue paper, or torn corrugated paper as I did, or cut them from a novelty fabric or lace. Then add narrow ribbons and other embellishments that suit the recipient and occasion. For the flowered ties, I simply slipped small paper flowers from a crafts supply shop onto some cord, tying a knot on each side of the flower as I did so, and spacing the blossoms about half an inch apart. For an elegant contrast to the corrugated paper, I glued some sparkly beads to the center of the large felt flower and also glued those pretty mirrored-glass blossoms to the package. The double gift tags are decorated with rubber stamp motifs.

Summer brights

Supplies: Wrapping papers – Tissue
paper – Newspaper – Thin ribbons –
Cords – Paper butterflies –
Curling ribbon – Felt flower cutouts –
Buttons – Gift tags – Scissors – Tape –
Glue gun & glue

Here is quite a variety of ideas! The packages with the butterflies and big bow made
of curling ribbon are wrapped as explained on
bottom of page 16. The yellow package and
wine bottle wrap are on page 23.

I've added wide sashes of contrasting paper
or tissue paper to the two packages at the
far right on the facing page, and topped them
with bands of everyday newspaper before
adding pretty ribbons threaded with felt
flower cutouts.

The button-trimmed packages are great
fun too. Choose any button with holes large
enough to thread some ribbon through, and
then let your imagination loose..

Delicious in citrus

Supplies: Wrapping papers – Computer, printer & colored paper – Regular & curling ribbons – Felt flower-decorated wire cord – Paper butterflies – Buttons – Gift tags – Scissors – Tape – Glue gun & glue

The yellow gift wrap with the green ribbon is unbelievably beautiful! I used shiny paper and wound a green silk ribbon several times around the box. I also found a wire string of felt flowers and green beads. The look couldn't be more complete.

I think the customized bottle is great for almost any occasion—you can use this idea for wine, as I did, or for anything that comes in a bottle or jar. All you need is an appropriate verse or saying and a computer. Choose the size of your label, type the verse to fit it, and print on colored paper. Then cut out, wrap around the bottle, and glue closed. Make a gift tag to match.

Turn to page 16 for directions for wrapping the packages with layered bands of paper on the facing page. I think they are fun with the printed butterflies as shown here, and of course they'd be charming with Christmas embellishments for your winter festivities.

If you love buttons, the package at right shows a unique way to use them! Just string onto several lengths of narrow ribbon or cord, and tie around your paper-wrapped box.

Colorful papers with colorful ribbons

Supplies: Wrapping papers – Ribbons – Cords – Scissors – Tape

It's the choice of wrappings that gives these presents their amazingly colorful look. The secret is to choose bright papers and then select ribbons and cords that repeat their hues—then you'll be set to go.

To get the full effect, it's important that your ribbons be of varying widths. When you wrap them around the package, weave them over and under each other and arrange them so some tie on each side.

Tip | The more varied your ribbon selection, the more amusing this gift wrap will be!

Congratulations!

Supplies: Wrapping papers – Metallic & angel-hair tissue papers – Corrugated paper – Ribbons – Strings of pearls – Fabric flowers – Small rhinestone buckles – Small trinkets – Gift tags – Scissors – Tape – Glue gun & glue

I think the package with the gorgeous big roses is just exquisite! Both the rose-patterned paper and the ribbon match the fabric roses so nicely. One rose, or two? Or use white paper bound with gold angel-hair tissue, cord, and roses. You decide.

The package with the teacup is lighthearted and perfect for an anniversary or wedding. Since many couples put dishes or silverware on their wish list, this is a fine way to hint at what's inside and it's certainly original!

The present with the heart-shaped arrangement of small, white fabric roses is incredibly sweet. Use solid-colored paper and then glue a strip of corrugated paper around the package so that the solid-colored paper peeks out at the ends. Then layer metallic tissue paper and mesh ribbon around the middle. Finally, glue small, white fabric roses all over the package or in a heart shape. Tie a heart or wedding ring trinket into the bow if you wish.

For the tailored packages on the facing page, I've used coordinating papers and embellished each with some ribbon, a sparkling buckle, and some pearls. When you choose buckles, look for the kind that slides on, without a prong.

Tip : Choose two or more papers with different patterns but the same colors so you can mix them creatively.

Janet

Jane

Springtime boxes

Supplies: Gift boxes, some with dish-like lids – Wrapping papers – Ribbons – Small fabric flowers – Buttons – Gift tags – Scissors – Glue gun & glue

Aren't these boxes pretty? I think both options offer a charming way to wrap a gift. I've wrapped the white boxes with handmade paper, covering the lids and bottoms separately. It's important to use plenty of glue for these. The lids are simply decorated with ribbons (tuck the ends under the rims) and a simple fabric flower. You might find other pretty embellishments around your home.

To make the button boxes, I've used scrapbook paper to decorate the bottom of the box and made the gift tag from the same paper. Patterned ribbons look sweet with these. I've been very generous in my use of buttons on the lid—the more the merrier! Use different shapes and sizes, but all in one color, and glue them into the depression in the lid, one on top of another.

Surprise, surprise

Supplies: Plain wrapping paper – Angel-hair tissue paper – Cellophane gift wrap – Heart & flower paper cutouts – Ribbons – Paper brads – Gift tag – Scissors – Tape

This gift wrap is a real surprise—when you open the layer of cellophane, dozens of small hearts fall out. You can buy die-cut paper motifs in all shapes and sizes, so choose whatever suits the occasion for the gift: Your imagination is the limit here. I first wrapped the box with a solid white paper and then covered that with a purple angel-hair tissue paper, which is slightly transparent. I scattered small heart cutouts in various colors and sizes on top of this before wrapping the whole thing in transparent cellophane—the hearts are contained, but move around when you shake the package. Finally, I tied two ribbons around the box and added a gift tag that I embellished with paper flowers held in place with little metal brads.

To Christine
From David

To Victoria
From Tim

A big envelope for a soft gift

Supplies: Wrapping paper – Self-adhesive Velcro – Sheer ribbon – Rickrack – Gift tag – Scissors

This is the perfect wrapping solution for things like sweaters. Lay an appropriately sized paper on your table and place the gift on it. Fold the edges of two opposite sides of the paper up and over onto the gift. Then, at one end, fold the perpendicular edge of the paper up and over, across the first two. Lastly fold up and crease a small margin along the remaining edge and then fold that edge up and over the gift, like the flap of an envelope. I used self-adhesive Velcro to hold the flap in place, you could use double-stick tape instead. For a fancy finish, I added both glittery sheer ribbon and some rickrack, and made coordinating gift tags.

A pretty flower says it all

Supplies: Wrapping papers – Ribbons – Fabric daisies & butterflies – Gift tags – Scissors – Tape – Glue gun & glue

Patterned paper paired with a patterned ribbon may appear a bit busy to some eyes, but I think it's fun to sometimes overdo things. For one of these presents, I tied a ribbon around each end of the package, glued a fabric Gerbera daisy in the middle of each ribbon, and tucked some fabric butterflies into the ribbons too. For the other package, I decided to use two ribbons together and tie the bow in an unusual place—on one narrow side, which became the top. I added two daisies by this bow, along with a tag made of black poster board. This style of wrapping is perfect for nearly any occasion—just choose colors, patterns, and posies that suit.

Queen of the dance

Supplies: Wrapping paper – Small fan – Peacock feathers – Half-mask – Rickrack –
Gift tag – Scissors – Tape – Glue gun & glue

Here's a theatrical gift wrap for the hostess of an elegant ball or similar festivity. Go to town with your choice of feathers—peacock like these, or perhaps iridescent coq. Or keep it really simple. Glue the feathers to the fan; then, if you like, paint or decorate the mask. I glued all the decoration diagonally at one corner of the box for a non-traditional effect. Now you are ready to pop the champagne cork!

Tip | Choose black wrapping paper—it will highlight the embellishments.

Cool combination

Supplies: Wrapping paper – Ribbons – Felt flower cutouts – Square beads or other baubles – Scissors – Tape – Glue gun & glue

Brown and turquoise is one of my favorite color combinations! So when I saw this paper I just had to have it. After wrapping the box, I cut a strip of the same paper, folded under its edges, and placed it diagonally around the box. Then I added velvet and sheer ribbons, felt flower cutouts, and bits of costume jewelry. Look for any trinkets that repeat the colors of your paper.

Chic wraps

Supplies: Patterned & plain wrapping paper – Raffia – Artificial flowers with wire stems –
Gift tags – Scissors – Tape

These show one of my favorite ideas. I used one kind of paper to cover the whole box and added a band of
another paper around the middle. Then I wrapped it with a bit of raffia and made a big bow. Finally, I twisted
the stems of some artificial flowers onto raffia in the same color, and added them around the whole package.

Summertime wrap for Mom

Supplies: Plain wrapping paper – Colored papers – Sheer ribbons – Raffia – Fabric butterflies – Scissors – Tape – Tabletop die-cutting machine & floral dies – Glue gun & glue

Mom will definitely appreciate these summery gift wraps. You'll find directions for the corrugated bags on page 42. For the pretty, scattered-flower packages, first, wrap the boxes in plain paper in order to show off the paper flowers, which I made using a die-cutting machine from a scrapbooking supplier. I chose flowers in different shapes and sizes, cut them from a variety of colored papers, and glued them randomly over the packages—overlapping them to create more interest. Several wraps of colorful ribbon tied in a bow could complete the effect, but I decided to take it a step further with big raffia bow and a fabric butterfly. These say "with love" for sure!

Naturally sweet totes

Supplies: Burlap – Corrugated paper – Assorted paper flowers – Ribbons – Gift tags –
Ruler – Scissors – Hole punch – Glue gun & glue

I got this wrapping idea while I was in Mexico City. I found some bags like these and when I got home I had
to see if it was possible to make something similar. It wasn't difficult at all.

First decide how large you want your bag to be. Cut a strip of burlap as long as needed to go around the bag
and as tall as you like. Then cut two strips of corrugated paper: Make both the same length as the burlap
strip but make one the height desired for the top border and one slightly more than twice the height desired
for the bottom border. Glue the long edges of the burlap to the corrugated paper strips. Then glue the ends
together to make a tube. Gently fold the bottom strip of corrugated paper to the middle of the tube, so the
edge overlaps slightly, then fold over the ends to form corners for the bottom of the bag. Secure the folded
sections with glue. Now you can begin decorating the bag as shown or however you wish.

For a special day

Supplies: Wrapping paper – Ribbon – Heart-decorated wire cord – Scissors – Tape –
Glue gun & glue

Imagine being surprised with a gift beautifully wrapped like the one on the facing page. It's perfect for
Mother's Day or someone's birthday—or any special day! I chose a truly lovely paper to cover the box, and
used a simple, plain ribbon that picks up one of the colors from the paper to wrap around it several times.
Then I dressed it up with a wire cord embellished with sweet, three-dimensional white hearts.

Gifts for her

Supplies: Wrapping papers – Scarves – Rhinestone buckles – Cord – Gift tags –
Scissors – Tape – Glue gun & glue

This is a clever wrapping because the recipient gets not one gift, but two. A beautiful scarf makes a great ribbon, and is a gift in itself. Cover the gift box with paper, then wrap the scarf around it in the usual cross or wrap it around in only one direction. Secure the scarf with a pretty buckle to make it even more exciting. Finally, attach the gift tag in the center of the package with a matching ribbon. I love the silvery, glittery elements I used, but bright primary hues could be fun too, or pastels would be sweet.

Festive gift wraps

Supplies: Wrapping papers – Silk papers or wide ribbons – Angel-hair tissue paper – Cord – Felt butterflies – Narrow ribbons – Small fabric flowers – Scissors – Tape – Glue gun & glue

I decorated the two boxes wrapped in sweet printed paper by circling each with a sash of handmade silk paper, which I gathered into a rosette that I secured with pretty cord. I finished the packages with cheery felt butterlies and gift tags I printed from my computer.

I crisscrossed the plum package with various ribbons and a band of angel-hair tissue paper, discreetly fastening them on the back with a bit of glue. The little handbag is a clever disguise for a girly gift; turn to page 59 to see how to make it.

Fancy cylinder & flask wraps

Supplies: Wrapping papers – Ribbons – Jute twine – Seasonal ornaments – Paper napkins with floral motifs – Decoupage medium – Small felt flower cutouts – Gift tags – Scissors – Glue gun & glue

I like things that can be recycled, and cylinders like the ones Pringles come in are handy for hiding gifts. Glue a bit of patterned paper around the cylinder. Then decorate it with ribbons at both ends or in the middle. I also cut out tags in matching colors and attached them, along with a cute seasonal ornament.

The color and design on the napkin you use for the cut-out motifs will make this fancy bottle appropriate for a summer gift or a Christmas present. To decorate the bottle, I first wound and glued some twine around it. If you pull the twine tightly as you go, you won't need to use much glue. Then I cut motifs from a paper napkin and fixed them to the twine with decoupage medium. I added little felt flowers to the gift tags; you could use any cutouts that complement your decoupage motif.

Bag it!

Supplies: Fabric – Small box (to be a mold for bottom of bag) – Felt cord – Small felt flowers – Gift tag – Scissors – Glue gun & glue

After much experimenting, I found an easy and ingenious way to make gift bags. The secret is to use a box the size desired for the bag bottom as a mold: Simply wrap canvas or a similar fabric around the box, making a tube that extends at the bottom slightly more than half the width of the box and at the top as much as you wish. Glue the overlapping vertical fabric edges together (but not to the box). Then fold and glue the bottom extension closed. Remove the box. It's a good idea to cut a bit of cardboard to reinforce the bottom of the bag. Make two holes near the top on one side of the bag, and then two more opposite them; thread the felt cord through them. Now you have a great gift bag that you can fill with whatever your heart desires.

Gifts for him

Supplies: Wrapping papers – Narrow ribbons – String – Snap hook or key ring – Gift tags – Travel ticket stubs or similar memorabilia – Scissors – Tape

Not many frills seen here: These are macho wrappings, but they could be softened up with a change of paper.

To be very tailored, wrap a box in dark brown paper or even kraft paper and wind a plain ribbon around it several times. Instead of tying a bow, fasten the ends to a snap hook or key ring.

To wish someone "bon voyage," use paper that looks like a world map—or use a road map or whatever else suggests a vacation or favorite destination of the recipient's. String instead of ribbon gives a nautical touch. I've attached some old ticket stubs and receipts from my last vacation. Of course, there's no reason not to use this for a woman with wanderlust too.

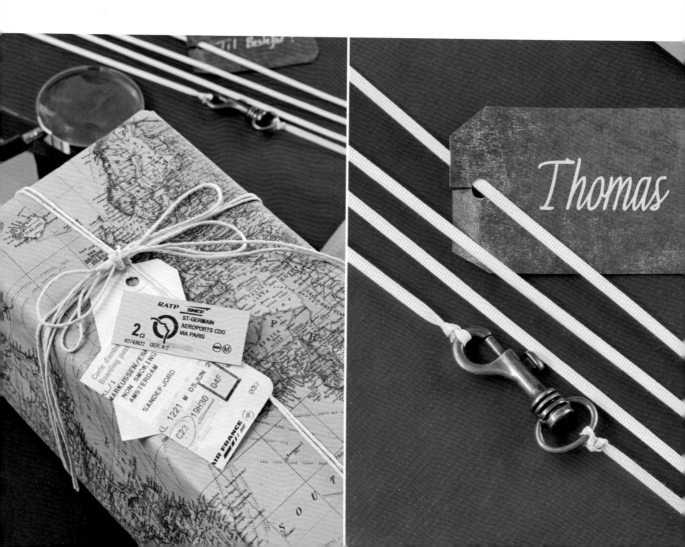

Tone-on-tone

Supplies: Wrapping papers – Angel-hair tissue paper – Ribbons – Small felt flower cutouts – Decorative cut-paper strip – Gift tags – Scissors – Tape

I used a wide band of angel-hair tissue to embellish the printed paper on the bottom two packages shown above, and added several satin ribbons around the angel-hair paper. I used some complementary paper to make gift tags. Turn to pages 46 and 47 to learn how I wrapped the top two packages. Note that I added a small band of cut paper to the one on the right; if you can't find something like this, make your own as you would paper dolls.

Mesmerizing

Supplies: Plain wrapping papers – Patterned circle cutouts – Buttons – Yarn or cord –
Scissors – Tape – Glue gun & glue

Here is a gift wrap for your Dad! Wrap the gift in any paper you like, for example blue or white as I've chosen.
Buy a packet of assorted die-cut circles (or cut your own from scraps of wrapping paper). Glue the circles
to the package—either next to one another or one on top of the other, arranging them as shown or in any
pattern you like. I glued buttons to the center of some of the circles too. Instead of ribbon, I used two
colors of yarn that match the colors of the circles, and held them together as I wrapped them around the
package and tied them in a simple bow. Mesmerizing, isn't it?

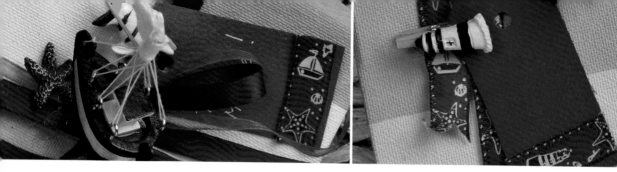

Wide blue sea

Supplies: Assorted wrapping papers or wallpapers, one with boat motif – Ribbons –
Nautical trinkets – Gift tags – Scissors – Tape – Glue gun & glue

A maritime theme makes these packages a perfect choice for a summer hostess gift or birthday. Wallpaper
is great for wrapping boxes, and that is what I've used here—the band with the sailboat motif is a border
strip. Craft supply and seaside gift shops are full of nautical trinkets, so you'll have plenty to choose from
when you look for embellishments to glue on. You can also use shells and other things you find along the
shore. I like the effect of the ribbons framing the edges of the sailboat border, don't you?

Whimsical tubes

Supplies: Wrapping papers – Printed paper plates – Colored cardstock – Ribbons – Scissors – Tape – Glue gun & glue

The beastly wraps in the middle below are fun to make for any gift that will fit into a cylinder—and fun to receive. To begin, cover the cylinder with plain or printed paper that works for whatever creature you have chosen to portray; then glue some bands of ribbon along its length. Use a child's funny paper plate for the head, gluing it at one end of the cylinder. Isn't that clever? Next cut out feet or something else from colored cardstock and glue them to the other end to help the cylinder balance. Add wing cutouts or dots or any other embellishment that suits. I love to use this ingenious presentation for a "sensible" gift.

All-occasion bags & boxes

Supplies: Paper shopping bags – Corrugated paper – Wrapping papers – Buttons – Regular & curling ribbons – Small toys – Gift tags – Scissors – Tape – Glue gun & glue

The shopping bag gift wraps were inspired by bags I saw in an exclusive children's boutique in Paris. For the top border, choose a colorful corrugated paper and cut one piece to fold over the top of the bag, making it as wide as the bag and twice the depth desired for the border. Now trim the edges in scallops or another decorative pattern. Next, fold the piece in half, unfold it, and cut a slit along the fold so that you can pull the handles through. Put your gift into the bag and slide the border over the handles; you can glue the border on if you wish.

I've also cut a big letter out of printed paper, decorated it with buttons, and glued it to the front—make the letter the recipient's initial. To make the bag extra-special, you can attach a ribbon and small toy or other trinket to the handle.

On the pink and turquoise packages, I've wrapped ribbons diagonally, around two of the corners, rather than in the traditional fashion. Glue the ribbons in the middle; then top the package with a big, curled ribbon bow and a cute toy that matches the paper. See page 59 to make the "purse" wraps.

The Seattle Public Library
Capitol Hill Branch
Visit us on the Web: www.spl.org

Check out date: 11/29/18

xxxxxxxxx4822

Wrap it up : 100s of fast, fun, and
0010074059493   Due date: 12/20/18
book

TOTAL ITEMS: 1

Renewals: 206-386-4190
TeleCirc: 206-386-9015 / 24 hours a day
Online: myaccount.spl.org

* * * * * * * * * * * * * * * * * * * *
Pay your fines/fees online at pay.spl.org

Rainbow wraps

Supplies: Plain wrapping or colored papers – Ribbons – Small toys or trinkets – Blank gift tags – Small letter stencils (optional) – Colored pencils or markers – Scissors – Tape – Glue gun & glue

Here is a fun presentation that is perfect for the little ones. I used regular construction paper instead of conventional wrapping paper, but either, or a mix, will do. Choose three different colors of paper and wrap the box in one of them. From each of the other colors, cut or tear a strip to go around the middle of the box, making one strip wider than the other. Glue the narrower strip along the middle of the wider one, and then glue or tape them around the box. Add ribbons and a small toy if you wish. Then decorate a gift tag with a colorful pattern of letters and numbers or any other motif you like.

Purse packages

Supplies: Wrapping papers – Ribbon or die-cut felt trims – Scissors – Tape – Glue gun & glue

This smart little purse may look complicated to make—but it's not. To begin, wrap the gift box in the usual way. Then cut a strip of wrapping paper for the handle, making it twice the width of the side of the box and as long as you like. Fold it in half lengthwise and glue closed. Glue the ends to the top of the box as shown. Next, cut a piece of paper for the flap, making it as wide as the package between the handle ends and as deep as you like (but at least deep enough to wrap over the top of the purse and hang down on the front). Decorate the flap with a band of ribbon and flowers—or anything that will please the girl who'll receive it—and then glue it in place between the handle ends.

Baby blue

Supplies: Two complementary wrapping papers – Ribbon – Small toy – Gift tag – Scissors – Tape – Glue gun & glue

With a different paper covering each half of the box, the package on the right, below, is twice as sweet. To do this easily, first wrap the entire box in one paper; then wrap half of it again using another paper. I combined a traditional printed paper with a special, handmade embroidered paper.

Once the paper is snug around the box, tie on a pretty ribbon, add a darling gift tag, and glue a small stuffed toy on top. Of course, you can use this idea for any occasion: I needed to wrap a christening gift, but your choice of paper and ribbons can make this idea right for any special gift.

Welcome, little one

Supplies: Plain wrapping papers – Paint pen – Ribbons – Small feathers – Small toy or trinket – Buttons with four holes – Gift tags – Scissors – Tape

I made the blue and pink "feather" papers myself! I simply wrote the text on colored paper with a paint pen. If you're not sure of your handwriting, practice first. This technique can be used for any occasion—you can convey the perfect sentiment, exactly as you wish, on this customized wrapping paper. Since these gifts are for a newborn, I wrote the word "feather" on the paper and glued small feathers with white ribbons randomly on the package. Finally, using the same ribbon, I tied a big bow and attached a pacifier. I think it's a super presentation for a newborn and mother. To wrap the button-trimmed packages, cut four pieces of ribbon—two for each direction. Lay them in a grid over the package, then thread them through four-hole buttons (make an X), and fasten each on the back of the package with a discreet dab of glue.

Doilies are great fun to use when decorating gift packages. Choose small ones, as I've done here, or larger ones, as suits the size of the box.

Valentine's gift wraps

Supplies: Wrapping papers - Tissue papers - Ribbons - Paper heart doilies -
Die-cut felt heart - Scissors - Tape - Glue gun & glue

If these packages don't signal romance, I don't know what does! They are wrapped with traditional wrapping paper, patterned tissue paper, and doilies—all decorated with heart motifs. To begin, choose a regular, opaque wrapping paper and wrap the gift. Then fold a piece of tissue paper around the package, either in the middle or over one end—I've done one of each here. Wrap and tie ribbons around the boxes. For embellishment, tuck some doilies under the tissue or ribbon, or thread doilies onto the ribbon tails.

Halloween gone wild

Supplies: Plain black & white wrapping papers – Sheer orange fabric – Black colored paper – Ribbons – Artificial cobwebs – Rubber bat – Gift tags – Scissors – Tape – Glue gun & glue

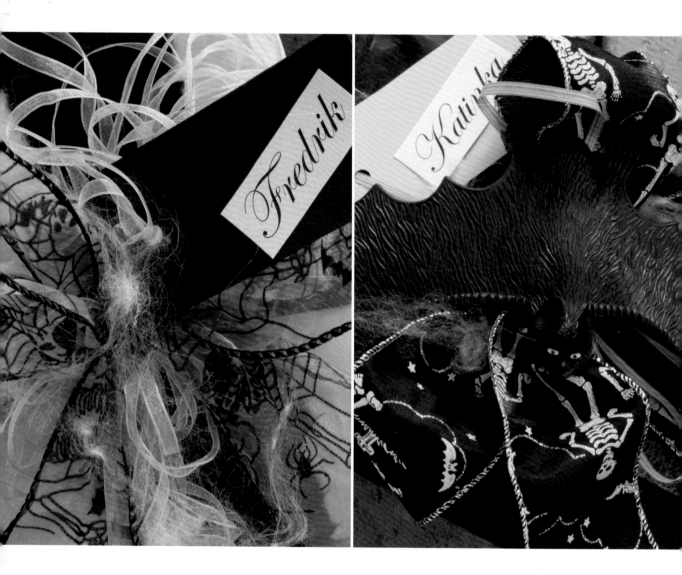

It's always nice to bring along a gift for your Halloween party host or hostess. I was inspired here by some "wicked" ribbons I found in Mexico. But you can find spooky trinkets almost anywhere during the Halloween season—fake cobwebs are a must for these gift wraps. One of these packages I wrapped in black paper and decorated with a skeleton-printed ribbon and thin, orange streamers. I also found a rubber bat that I think adds the perfect touch.

For the other package I used white paper first, then covered it with sheer orange fabric. To break up the field of orange colors, I tore a little strip of black colored paper and wrapped it like a sash around the middle. Then I was very generous with my use of both the wider, spider-printed ribbon and the skinny orange one. All that's missing is "trick or treat?"

Coffee tins & lidded gift boxes

Supplies: Computer, printer & paper – Metal canister – Wrapping papers – Angel-hair tissue paper – Die-cut felt ribbons – Assorted ribbons & cords – Gift tags – Scissors – Tape – Glue gun & glue

If you have a computer and printer, you can make your own labels for a gift of coffee or tea—the perfect present for the person who has everything. I found this fun metal tin with a window on the front into which you can slip your own label. I filled it with coffee and added a label I designed and printed myself. I also filled a plain brown bag with coffee at my local specialty market and then glued my label onto it. Use your imagination to design a label that suits the contents or the recipient. This present smells great too!

For a special wrap that can be reused, choose a box with a lid. Perhaps you have a shoebox around; if not, you can purchase a lidded gift box. For these, I used solid-colored paper on the boxes and a coordinating patterned paper on the lids. I cut a strip of delicate tissue paper and wrapped it around the middle of the box. I found a terrific wide, die-cut ribbon made of thick felt, wrapped it over the tissue, and tied a thinner ribbon on top. Embellishments cut from the felt ribbon accent the gift tags and some other, classically wrapped, packages.

Let it snow; let it snow . . .

Supplies: Wrapping papers – Thin metallic cords – Acrylic snowflakes – Gift tags –
Scissors – Tape

Here I wrapped three different presents of varying sizes in the same paper—but in different colors! Imagine
how beautiful they will look under a Christmas tree. Wrap the cord many times around the package to create
a delicate, sparkling sash; then embellish your work with a big, glittering snowflake and a matching tag.

Jingle bells, jingle bells . . .

Supplies: Two coordinating wrapping papers – Raffia – Thin metallic cord – Small bells –
Gift tags – Scissors – Tape – Glue gun & glue

These silver and white gift wraps are a treat for the eye! I think the paper looks very Nordic, but I actually found it in London. The secret to these is the ripped, layered strips of contrasting paper: First wrap the box in one paper. Then instead of cutting, rip the contrasting paper into strips and glue them around the package. Wrap one or two lengths of raffia around the package and tie them in a bow; add silver bells hung on silver cord. To finish, I made tags from silver poster board. I think the result is a wrapping that is off-beat but very stylish, and unique.

Yuletide elegance

Supplies: Wrapping papers – Mesh & solid ribbons – Die-cut felt ribbon – Cords – Star-decorated wire cord – Seasonal trinkets – Scissors – Tape – Glue gun & glue

The top two packages on the facing page are beautiful and delicate, yet simple to make. The effect you achieve depends upon which papers you choose—glossy papers like these are very dressy. Wrap the present in the paper you want to use as a base. Then cut a band of the second paper and wrap it around the middle of the package. Place a narrower band of the first paper over this—you can fold pleats into it if you like. Next add some lovely ribbons or cords, and some stars cut from felt, another paper, or whatever you like.

To wrap the two gifts on the bottom of the facing page, I pleated a large sheet of paper before covering the box: Start with a sheet considerably larger than you would need for a flat wrapping. Place it face up on your table and begin to fold pleats into it—you can decide whether you want the pleats to be straight, slanted, or even fanned. On the package covered with solid red paper, I tucked a strip of patterned paper into the folds. Fancy ribbon tied in simple bows and holiday embellishments complete these pretty packages.

Quick special effects

Supplies: Double-sided wrapping papers – Ribbons – Christmas ornaments – Tassels –
Scissors – Tape – Glue gun & glue

I found the wrappings for all these gifts at IKEA (look online if you don't have a store nearby). The paper is double-sided—printed with a different pattern on each side—so there are lots of possibilities. When I wrapped the boxes, instead of having the seam at the bottom of the package, I placed it on top, and left an extra-large overlap so I could fold the paper back to show off the opposite side. Matching Christmas ornaments and shimmering tassels provide the perfect finishing touch.

Harmony in black & gold

Supplies: Glossy plain wrapping paper – Corrugated paper – Ribbons – Gift tag –
Scissors – Tape

This present is hot! It's perfect for a sophisticated friend for Christmas or a birthday. I used shiny, black wrapping paper to create an exclusive appearance. Then I tore a length of gold corrugated paper and wrapped it around the package. Finally, I added some ribbons in black and gold. Très chic!

Dreams in blue & gold

Supplies: Wrapping paper – Angel-hair tissue paper – Metallic ribbon – Metallic cord –
Sheer fabric leaves – Holiday greetings cutouts – Scissors – Tape – Glue gun & glue

Christmas doesn't always have to be red and green. Sometimes I see wrapping paper I just have to have—
even though I have no idea what I'll use it for. This leaf print is one of those papers. It's handmade with
acid-washed leaves that have been embedded in the paper itself. To enhance the effect on the larger
package, I added a layer of angel-hair tissue to one end, and covered the join with gold ribbons and cord. I
also bought a few loose gold leaves to embellish the ribbons. I think these Christmas packages are a dream.

Noel!

Noel!

Tip Simplicity pays the best compliment to beautiful handmade trims, so choose a plain paper and unprententious twine for these wrappings.

From my mother

Supplies: Wrapping papers – Handmade crochet ribbon & heart – Jute twine – Seasonal trinkets – Gift tags – Small safety pins – Scissors – Tape

My mother is the world's best when it comes to crochet! So she helped me with the gift wraps on the facing page. There are many crochet patterns available online or in booklets, but if crochet isn't your thing, you can find similar trims readymade. If you make your own, measure the box first to see how long to make each piece. I'm sure you agree with me: Handmade trims are something special.

Wrap your gift in the paper. Wrap the crocheted trim around the package and pin it on the bottom (pins won't damage the trim). I used rather thick jute twine to tie up these packages, and in place of a bow, I cut several 8-inch lengths and glued them in the center. I cut simple paper gift tags and applied one to the middle of the crocheted heart, the other to a purchased ornament.

Elfin delights

Supplies: Wrapping paper – Crepe paper – Yarn or twine – Gift tags – Scissors – Tape

The packages on this page are intended to look a bit old-fashioned, and they can be made in a jiffy! I paired a printed wrapping paper with a solid-color crepe paper. Wrap your gift in one and then cut two bands of the other to place around it like a cross. Tape them in place on the package back. Then wrap the yarn around the package, passing it under the top band, tie it in a simple bow, and finish it off with a handmade gift tag.

A cold winter's night

Supplies: Wrapping paper – Ribbons – Small metal snowflakes – Gift tags –
Scissors – Tape – Glue gun & glue

Snowflakes are beautiful, and each is as unique as
you are! This Christmas wrapping is lovely to look
at, and it's fun to use colors other than the traditional reds and greens. I think the velvet ribbons
are key to the great look of these packages. You
can use two or three rows in each direction around
your package—more if you like. Cut a separate
length for each row. Place the ribbons around the
package in one direction first, tying or gluing them
on the bottom. When you place the ribbons in the
other direction, weave them into the first ones.
Embellish your gift tags with a bit of ribbon and
some metal snowflakes.

Dreaming of a white Christmas

Supplies: Wrapping paper – Raffia – Pom-poms – Gift tags – Scissors – Tape – Glue gun & glue

If this wrapping isn't cool, I don't know what is! I began with extremely clever paper—very Norwegian, really. I tied the packages with simple raffia and then scattered pom-poms around the surface and glued them on. I'd set out to use smaller pom-poms here, but the store only had large ones. I think the wrapping turned out great anyway. Plain gift tags are the right choice for this wrap. Now these packages are ready to go under the tree.

Then & now

Supplies: Wrapping papers – Ribbons – Fancy trims – Photos – Non-permanent glue stick –
Gift tags – Trinket-decorated wire cords – Scissors –Tape – Glue gun & glue

Gift wraps that include photographs are very special, both to receive and to give! I've used some photos that belonged to my grandmother, but of course you could just as well use pictures of the kids' summer vacation. For the wrappings on this page and the bottom of the facing page, I covered the boxes with paper and then tied them with ribbons—wrapping the ribbon in one direction on some, and around the corners on the others. Then I chose positions for the photos and applied them with a temporary glue stick so the recipient can remove them without tearing them. Directions for the box with the pleated paper wrapping are on page 71.

For the gift wraps at the top of the facing page, I used two complementary papers. After wrapping the box in one paper, I cut a tapered strip of the other one, folded under its edges, and glued it at a jaunty angle across the package. Those great decorated wire cords add a festive finish—you can find them embellished with all sorts of seasonal shapes and they're fun to bend into position.

Woof, woof!

Supplies: Wrapping papers – Ribbons – Raffia – Dog biscuits & treats – Gift tags – Scissors – Tape

Christmas only comes once a year, and a four-legged family member is as deserving of a little gift for the big holiday as the rest of us. Use a paper with an appropriately canine print. Tie some great coordinating ribbons and raffia around the package and embellish it with some dog biscuits you can find at the pet shop. Fido will be happy when you unwrap it for him and pass out the treats!

To Kate

For Tom

Snowbound

Supplies: Wrapping paper – Angel-hair tissue paper – Die-cut felt ribbons – Gift tags – Scissors – Tape

The presents below are for my father and my brother; no fuss, no frills. For the one on the right, I added a strip of the same paper that I wrapped it in to the middle and then wrapped two rows of great die-cut snowflake ribbon around it. To contrast the light blue paper, I placed a band of red angel-hair tissue paper around the box on the left and wrapped a red die-cut ribbon over that. I decorated the gift tags with motifs cut from the ribbons.

Bottles of cheer

Supplies: Fabrics – Ribbons & trims – Small trinkets – Scissors – Glue gun & glue

A bottle of wine or fancy vinegar makes a nice gift for a hostess or someone who needs nothing in particular. A fancy wrap like the ones on the facing page makes the presentation festive. Start with a square of fabric with a diagonal measurement several inches longer than the bottle's height. Place the bottle diagonally on it, and roll it up; secure the fabric to itself with some glue. Then fold the fabric neatly onto the bottom of the bottle and glue. Fold the fabric down at the top and secure by tying some ribbon around the neck of the bottle. Add some holiday trinkets and a gift tag.

Gift-on-gift

Supplies: Wrapping paper – Cord – Ornament or piece of jewelry – Gift tag –
Scissors – Tape

This wrapping is extremely easy to make, yet so festive. I love that the embellishment itself serves as an extra gift for the lucky recipient. The jeweled star is a Christmas ornament; use anything similar, preferably with small loops at the points (or spaced along the edge if it's not a star). I wrapped the gift box with plain red paper. Then I cut lengths of gold cord, threaded them through the rings at the star points, centered the star on the package, and tied the cords snugly on the other side. If you can't thread cord through your ornament, tie a doubled cord around your box and then glue on the ornament. I made the gift tag myself, decorating it with a whimsical cutout.

For the one you love

Supplies: Wrapping paper –Ribbon – Large die-cut felt hearts – Scissors –
Tape – Glue gun & glue

The packages on the facing page are simple and also very stylish, with the ribbon taking center stage. I like the mix of solid-color paper with such a special bow. To make it, tie the ribbon around the package, making a simple knot with two streamers. Then cut another length of ribbon and roll it up into a spiral. Set the spiral on its side and secure it by gluing between the layers. Then glue it to the top of your package. The gift tags are attached to filigree felt hearts, which you can buy at most craft supply stores.

To Inger Elise
From Unni

TO MARY
FROM OLAF

Tip ⋮ Use a die-cut felt shape as part of your gift tag. It's a
present itself, which the recipient can hang on her tree.

Starry, starry night

Supplies: Wrapping paper – Metallic tissue paper – Metallic ribbon – Metallic star cutouts –
Gift tags – Scissors –Tape – Glue gun & glue

These are beautiful Christmas packages that shine as brightly as the stars. I wrapped one of them in white
paper. I wrapped the other, larger, one in metallic gold tissue paper that I first crushed for a nice effect. I
tied them both with ribbon and then I glued stars of various sizes to the packages. You can buy the stars at
a crafts supply store.

Chic & trendy

Supplies: Wrapping papers – Corrugated paper – Ribbons – Large beads – Beading wire –
Gift tags – Scissors – Tape – Glue gun & glue

These packages may not look like typical Christmas presents, but they are definitely full of good cheer. I found the light blue paper on a visit to New York. It is double-sided and so is easy to mix and match. But there are lots of coordinated papers available, even if you can't find any double-sided options locally.

I embellished the blue packages with bands of red corrugated paper that I topped with ribbon. To create the wave effect, I simply looped the ribbon over my finger and glued it down at regular intervals.

You can experiment to see if additional ribbon or a different type of bow adds to the fun of your package. I also used pieces of the same wrapping paper to make the gift tags.

The red packages are similarly assembled, but the contrasting bands are strips of wrapping paper instead of corrugated paper. For one of the red packages I folded a diagonal pleat in the paper before covering the box with it. I strung the gift tags on wire, along with some cool beads.

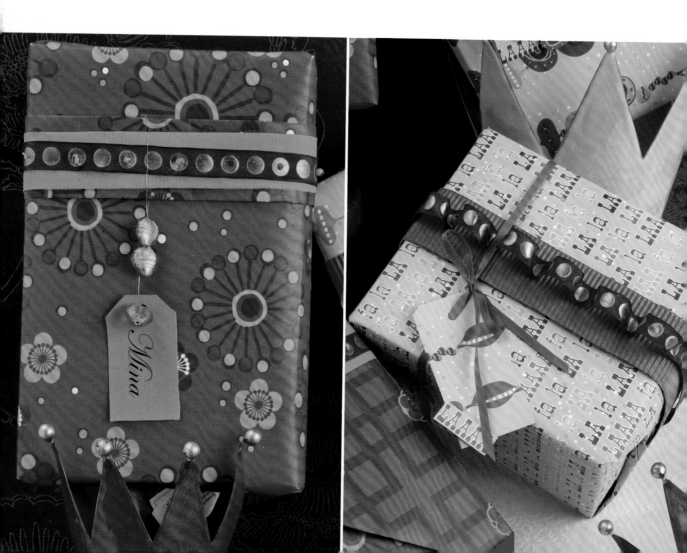

Golden sparkler

Supplies: Metallic tissue paper – Wide sheer ribbon – Metallic ribbons –
Small clear glass ornaments – Small metallic trinkets – Scissors – Tape

The package on the facing page is so beautiful on its own, it doesn't even need to contain a gift! It's a wonderful wrapping that is guaranteed to attract attention on any gift table. I wrapped the box first with crumpled metallic gold tissue paper and placed a wide, gold sheer ribbon around the middle. Then I added all sorts of shiny gold ribbons and trinkets and tucked some clear ornaments among the tendrils, where they sparkle as they catch the light!

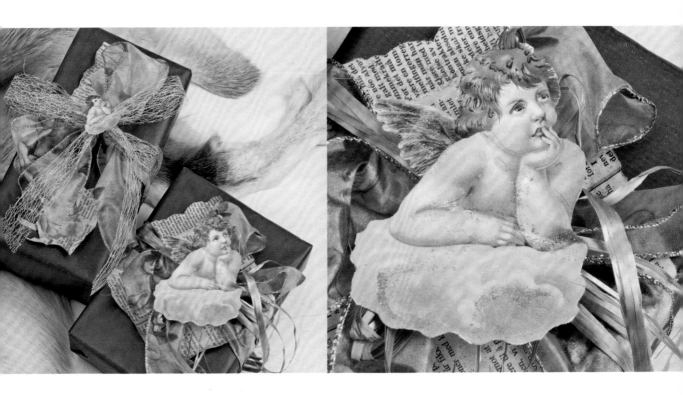

Angel to angel

Supplies: Plain wrapping paper – Newspaper – Nostalgic angel paper cutouts – Ribbons –
Glitter glue – Scissors – Tape – Glue gun & glue

These small packages give nostalgia a modern twist. To make them, first wrap the box in plain paper. Tear a strip of newspaper in the size you want and decorate it with glitter glue. Glue the newspaper to the center of the package and tie a complementary ribbon around it. Finally, glue a classic, vintage angel cutout to the top.

Wrapping basics

You are encouraged to put your own spin on every gift wrap shown in this book—they'll be lovely even if you use different kinds of paper or ribbon.

Nearly any kind of paper can be used. Tissue paper is sheer; you may need to put a heavier, white paper under it to obscure any color or pattern on the gift box. Glossy paper tends to show any misplaced creases, so handle it thoughtfully.

Cut the wrapping paper large enough to overlap and fold under the edges, but not so large that the overlaps are bulky.

Wrap the paper around the box, placing the overlapping seam on one edge on the bottom.

You can secure the paper with tape or glue. Double-stick tape and glue both give the neatest results. I like to use hot glue. Glue sticks are good too—they're not messy.

Look for ribbons in fabric stores as well as at a stationery store. You can also use lace, strips of tulle or organza, yarn, crochet thread, twine or string from the hardware store, or home furnishings trims. I love to use those delicate embellished wire garlands sold with holiday wrapping papers. There are so many options! Ribbon and other trim can be costly, so plan ahead.

Buttons, paper and fabric flowers, die-cut motifs, and other small embellishments add a lot to a gift wrap. Check out the scrapbooking department in crafts and art supply stores as well as the trimmings department in a fabric store. Don't forget tassels and glitter!

A custom-made gift tag is a wonderful addition to any present. There are templates for a variety of tags on page 96. Use a craft knife to cut them from cardstock or other heavy paper. You can glue wrapping paper or tissue paper to the cardstock if you like. You'll see lots of ideas for decorating tags in the photos in this book, and you will no doubt have ideas of your own too. For fancy lettering, type the message on your computer and print it on colored paper.

Fido!

Gift tag templates

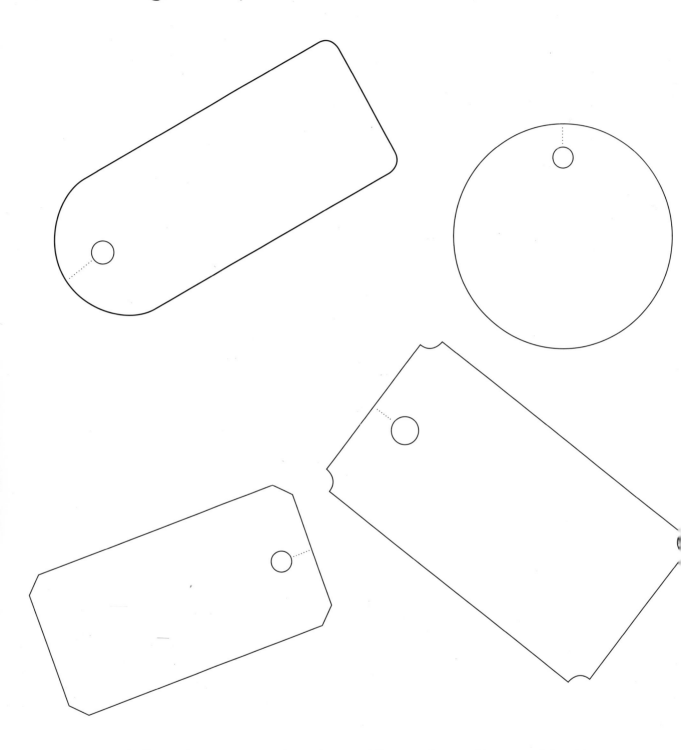

Tip — Cut the tag on the dotted line—from the end to the hole—so that you can easily slip it onto the ribbon when you're finished wrapping the gift.